Math *by*

Grace

Memorization of Basic Math for
Concentration-Challenged Children
through Relaxation and Meditation Techniques

Dana Williams

Attunement Press

The contents of this book do not constitute a prescription or treatment recommendation.

Dedicated in gratitude to Joe Koperski,
who taught white light meditation to me
when I was still very young

Content

Author's Note

I had no idea how much of a role math played in the lives of my children, or how disheartening it was for them to get low test results in school until, later, (after doing *Math by Grace*), they would come home proud, glowing, and overwhelmed with joy at their grades. They said their position in class was improving along with their math test scores. They had greater self-esteem.

Another role that math plays: If SAT math scores are low, college options may be limited. Parents therefore often begin working on math with their kids at a young age, playing games that encourage math skills, drilling, or enrolling their children in a math tutoring center. But sometimes a child just does not get it.

This book is not your usual math book, as it is written for parents or therapists *who have devoted themselves to a practice that promotes calm and relaxation such as relaxation exercises, yoga, Qigong, T'ai Chi, meditation, or other similar practice.* If you have worked to increase your inner calm and focus, this book may show you a way to communicate this calm to your child through a guided visualization for math.

If you do not have such a background but would like your child to be guided in *Math by Grace*, try to find a yoga teacher, therapist or child specialist to act as your child's MBG guide. Perhaps this person will go on to help many more children in your area.

I developed *Math by Grace* with my own children in 1998 as a reaction to nothing else working for them—not drills, games, or explanations. The first time I tried *Math by Grace* I did not know what to expect. I viewed the amazing results suspiciously—but at the same time was so grateful! First one child and then the next went to the top of their class in no time at all. Then my autistic child (he was speaking three word sentences at five years of age) improved exponentially with only one *Math by Grace* session. I was floored. I sat in front of my computer for three full days and did nothing else but write up the approaches I had taken with my children, for each had received a slightly different version of *Math by Grace*, tailored to fit the individual child's age and attention span.

Of course, there is no guaranty that *Math by Grace* will improve every child's basic math memorization. Many factors play together, such as the number of hours a child spends in front of a television or computer, and the child's quality of diet and exposure to neuro-exciting additives and toxins. But at the very least the process of relaxation and visualization, and of working towards a state of mental calm and control, can provide your child with an inner experience that may be unexpectedly fruitful in many areas of life. *Math by Grace* can never equal a loss!

I completed my original manuscript in the hope that it might help other parents who are struggling to support their talented but concentration-challenged young children. That was ten years ago, and my children are now grown. Their math skills are good. One child is even considered gifted. With pleasure, I return to my notes.

In publishing this book I wish to share with parents, therapists and teachers what I discovered, how it led to my developing *Math by Grace*, and how that practice affected the lives of my children. In this book you will find information and insights that will hopefully enable you to create a relaxation, visualization and exercise program just right for you and your special child or children.

This book is a "first edition" of what will hopefully be many future, and improved versions. I would like to hear from you: based on your own background and life experiences, what exactly did you try with your child, and how did it work? Also, are there sections of this book that were difficult to understand? Do you need more information or explanation in any area?

Please use the contact address on page 72 to send me your comments and experiences of *Math by Grace*. I look forward to hearing from many parents and children!

Dana Williams   April 2009

Part One

Background

As you read this book, you may find yourself admitting that you sometimes add and subtract on your fingers or that you have forgotten your multiplication tables—if you ever really knew them. This would have described me, until the day I sat down to think about my children's struggles with math. Then began an adventure that allowed me to train my own math mind. Suddenly, I was great at basic math. I could easily add up the groceries as I put them in the cart, or know exactly what I would pay for a combination of dishes ordered at a restaurant.

Ironically, as I looked through childhood memorabilia not long ago, I ran across an IQ test from the fifth grade. I would never have believed it—my strongest ability was math!

Why wasn't my math ability developed?

I think I was one of the early Indigos—high strung and creative, intuitive, courageous, and feeling as though I was born to change the world. But none of that worked for math. In the first grade, I designed a way to add and subtract without having to concentrate. I pictured the numbers like dots on the sides of dice. As I added up the numbers, I poked my pencil onto the paper, counting imaginary dots one by one. *I did not realize that the goal would have been to jump over the counting step.* Forget the dots! Forget your fingers! Forget counting! The goal was to *memorize* basic math—to learn it "by heart."

But what does learning "by heart" mean?

Can the heart learn math?

Learning "by heart" implies "memorization." Memorization requires that we temporarily block out the world and concentrate wholly within ourselves. It requires that we engrave the thing to be learned on some part of our inner being that we can later access effortlessly at will. Exactly how this happens, no one knows—but our language suggests that it has something to do with the heart.

In western culture, we assume that knowledge is stored in the brain, an organ that has often been compared to machines or to computers to illustrate its ability to function and perform tasks. We also say that our deeper emotions live in the heart. Anything "heartfelt" is sincere: we have "heartache" when we are worried and "heartbreak" when we grieve a loss "whole-heartedly." We also have gut-feelings, or intuitions, called "emotional IQ." Neural transmitters in the intestine act in a similar way to neural transmitters in the brain. The result of the gut's processing is a kind of emotional information, such as happiness, contentment, nausea, butterflies, repulsion, or "feeling sick to my stomach."

Our western concepts about thoughts, deep emotions and gut feelings are quite different from perceptions in the east. For instance, in ancient China it was believed that we think with our heart and that we feel with our stomach. The head, the home of the six senses, was thought capable of perceiving the world but not of reflecting upon it. The Chinese reasoned that whereas the senses, such as the eyes and ears, can be fooled and beguiled, the heart's "mind" may be cultivated: it can become calm enough to evaluate experience fairly and to think things through thoroughly.

In Chinese literature, the heart is portrayed as having both an immature and a potentially mature nature. It is first of all a center of strong emotion such as joy, grief, sorrow or disappointment. After being cultivated and refined, it becomes capable of tranquility, deep thought, understanding and wisdom—and presumably also of memorization (learning "by heart").

Children today have problems concentrating. Environmental toxins, habits of diet and media consumption all work against our children (and their parents) developing a calm heart and thus a calm mind. This shows itself in school results, especially where memorization is required, as in spelling or math. However, if the child's parent has worked on some kind of calming discipline, she may be able to transfer that calm to her child—by shared experience with visualization and concentration exercises. This transfer can take place with particular poignancy during the *Math by Grace* session.

The phrase "learn by heart" describes an inward turning of concentration, a moment when the body and the mind are working together without distraction. There is complete focus. We are one with ourselves. We are centered in our heart, and our mind is free to learn well.

How I Developed MBG with my Kids

Each of my four children had a hard time memorizing their basic math. This lack was painfully obvious when it came time to learn their multiplication tables in primary school. If I asked them a somewhat harder problem, such as 6 x 7, they took it as an invitation to begin an endless guessing game. I was convinced that my kids had at least average intelligence, but when it came to basic math, each of them seemed far below average.

When Michael, my oldest and most intellectually brilliant son began to fail at school at age 11, I had him evaluated. He tested with an IQ of 133. That's the lower range of genius. But while his scores in language and abstract thinking were off the charts he had a below average score in structural thinking.

Today, this kind of imbalance is not unusual. The psychologist who tested Michael explained that many gifted children have problems with math and do poorly in school. She said that because everyday life has become so complex, smart children begin to assess and solve difficult problems from the time they are very young. She said that when complexity is the norm, the simplicity involved in memorization becomes difficult. For the brains of these children, memorization equals a waste of time!

⇨ Kids today are used to dealing with complexities. They have little patience to learn basic structural tools of learning such as memorization.

My second son was a natural athlete and artist: he loved sports, singing, drawing, writing and filmmaking. Like my first son, he just couldn't memorize the multiplication tables. All his energies were creative and spontaneous, and he found no spontaneous, creative way to approach memorization.

My third child had a developmental delay and rather severe learning problems: he did not speak in three-word sentences until he was five. He was evaluated as having above average intelligence, however, (yes, this is possible), and by age ten was able to use language well. However, even in a small, special education class, and under the guidance of a specially trained teacher, he just could not learn those danged multiplication tables!

My forth child and only daughter is both creative and above-average intelligence. She was constantly on the go. I knew that if we were living in the city, rather in the country where she had a free range of movement, she would have been diagnosed as having attention deficit hyperactivity disorder and we would have been advised to put her on Ritalin. Nonetheless, I was expecting that she, of all my children, would have no problem with math at school because she practiced it with enthusiasm as a toddler—sitting in on my lessons with her brothers and learning to give the answers. But when she entered school, sure enough, she just could not memorize those danged multiplication tables.

It was so frustrating! My efforts at home such as verbal repetition, daily written exercises, and math games with cards just did not make the material stick. I was at a loss.

Then I developed an approach that enabled my children, in no time at all, to become proficient in the multiplication tables and in division. The material stuck and the child began to excel at math. Even though my children have different degrees of aptitude for math, and each has a different kind of concentration problem, they each quickly improved. We experienced no more frustration. No more failure. The real fruit of this work though was their heightened self-esteem. The fact that they moved up in their class in math meant a great deal to them.

Frustrated with Old Methods

First off, I have to mention that I did not implement MBG with Michael—my son with an IQ of 133. Michael had struggled though years of frustrating attempts at memorization with daily written exercises, verbal repetition and flash cards. In the meantime, his math grades were poor and his self-esteem was suffering.

Michael did eventually memorize his multiplication tables on his own in the sixth grade—too late to help his self-esteem. He was never enthusiastic about higher math and he continued to find it difficult into adulthood. Michael was in already in early puberty when I developed *Math by Grace* for his younger brother, Pascal. He was no longer willing to "learn with Mom." I respected his resistance. It just was not to be.

Perhaps you will have more luck with your child who is already in puberty. Let me know! The message I want to convey to you though now is this: please, never force a child to use this method. A child has to be willing to open their heart to learn by heart. If your child isn't willing to enter that "space" with his parent or guardian look for someone (yoga teacher, therapist or child specialist) the child feels more comfortable with to be his MBG guide. Otherwise, let it be.

Brain-Storming for a New Method

Shortly after my younger son, Pascal, complained about not being good at math in the third grade, I discovered a book in a used-book store: "Give Your Child a Superior Mind," by Siegfried and Therese Engelmann, published in 1966 by Simon and Schuster. The author, Siegfried Engelmann, a Research Associate at the Institute for Research on Exceptional Children at the University of Illinois, worked mainly with culturally disadvantaged children, including deaf, mentally retarded, and gifted children. His wife and co-author, Therese Engelmann, was a child psychologist and his partner in research.

The Engelmanns worked with a wide range of disadvantaged and challenged children, and they reported success with each group. As I read into the book, I discovered that the learning processes they described jived with my own learning experiences as a musician. I describe this on page 53.

The Engelmanns portray the young child's mind as a dark expanse of catacombs or caves that become illumined the more the child understands about the world. As the child makes sense out of life, she lays tracks in her mind to remind her of what she has learned. These tracks (or neural connections) are the routes that the child's thoughts will travel in the future. If the tracks are laid out in clear, direct patterns, learning and recall will be easy. The child can excel. If they are laid out in crisscrossed, mixed-up patterns, the child will have problems learning and remembering.

The Engelmanns endorse simplifying a learning process to its core essence. For instance, no cute animals should be drawn onto the letters of the alphabet to make them more appealing to the child. That is already too much information that has nothing to do with the actual matter at hand. And don't tell human-interest stories while teaching math. Stay with the pure lesson. The Engelmanns maintain that by keeping the lessons as simple and clear as possible, the initial tracks the child lays down will be clear, clean, and direct, and that subsequent learning will be greatly excelled in speed and easy grasp of complexities.

The Engelmanns were convinced that every child is born with the potential to learn, even to be a genius—if she can just get her tracks set right from the get-go. "The function of a preschool education is not so much to teach the child specific facts, as it is to direct his track-laying efforts...."

Learning efficiently means developing the ability to go inwards with calm resolve and to lay down tracks well. This is what I call "learning by heart." It entails being in the non-judgmental, fearless state of mind that we effortlessly obtain when we are close to Self.

The goal of early education is therefore not so much to learn specific things as it is to teach the child the most effective process of learning. If we can learn without stress and with good recall, we will be able to enjoy and expand our intellectual powers.

You have probably seen illustrations of nerves developing in a baby's brain in response to stimuli from the environment. Beginning when the baby is born, these nerves branch out from the brain's center, looking somewhat like an entanglement of seaweed. They continue to grow throughout childhood and adolescence, with occasional stops, rewinds, and fast-forwards, filling out most of the brain.

Researchers say that the way that these branches grow in early life will have a profound influence on a child's development. At first, a great multitude of tracks reflect the child's spontaneous exploration of life. But as the child grows older, tracks disappear. Only those tracks remain that are used often, so that the brain of an eighteen-year-old typically has fewer tracks than that of a two-year-old. And yet, throughout our lives we can develop and use new tracks. We never lose the ability to learn.

Wouldn't it be great if children could delete old, wrongly laid tracks—tracks that lead nowhere or that lead only round in circles—and lay new ones entirely? This is possible with *Math by Grace*: relaxation, meditation, deep breathing, and guided visualization allow children to be rid of the old and to lay new tracks.

A good analogy for track laying is the old-fashioned record player. When Thomas Edison first successfully recorded sound, he set a needle to vibrate (make grooves or tracks) in a hard but waxy substance. In this analogy, think of sound, or vibration, as *real life experience*. The needle is the calm heart, steadily recording the experience. After it is recorded, it will again require a calm needle set neatly into a groove to accurately pick up whatever is recorded there.

We need a calm heart both to memorize and to recall.

Simply put, grooves are engraved in the mind to record what we learn and experience. But if the needle (concentration) is not steady, the recording will be scratchy and the music of memory will be full of static. If we can hold the needle steady—if we can find and cultivate the tranquil concentration of the heart—the experience recorded on the brain will result in beautiful, rich sound, full of useful information.

> If the needle is not set steady in the math learning process, when we later ask "How much is 9 x 7?" all the child's mind will hear is static.

To return to my personal story, each of my four children got their math-grooves full of scratches while at school. When I'd ask my child "How much is 9 x 7?" my child's mind would jump from "I knew that yesterday," to "If I wrack my brains it'll come to me," to "How can I figure this out... now, 9 x 5 is 40, plus 9 x 2 is....oh, no, where was I?"

After reading "Give Your Child a Superior Mind," I recognized this static for what it was.

The Englemanns explain that:

- *If a track is laid directly from a question to its answer,* in a moment of calm "learning by heart," the answer appears effortlessly—lightning fast. Before you finish asking the question, it is already there.

- The answer is so direct that it does not even have to be called up. There is no wracking of brains or trying to recall how this kind of problem is solved. The answer seems magically to appear.

My math-challenged kids clearly did not have tracks laid directly from a question to an answer. Their messed-up tracks took them here, there, anywhere but to the place where the sure and certain answer lay. And the more they wracked their brains, the farther away they found themselves from the answer they sought.

According to the Engelmanns, the problem of poorly laid tracks is compounded by the expectation of failure. Children who have negative learning experiences learn to expect that they will fail. Rather than confidently going for the answer, an inner voice says "I can't, I can't." Even if a question is easy and the child knows the answer, she may give the wrong answer instead—to fulfill the expectation of failure.

Children need to hear from people they trust that they are smart. Their expectation of failure has to change before they can begin to successfully learn and recall what they learn.

When I realized that my second son, just like my first, could not memorize basic math, I began to think about our predicament. I realized I had to somehow find a way to *undo the static,* to *set the needle freshly onto my child's mind.*

Then I read the following paragraphs in Engelmann's book, and a light went on for me:

> "A child in a stress situation tends to repeat the same mistakes, over and over (like Michael had). The more vehemently you try to extinguish the incorrect response, the more persistently he will hang onto it....
>
> "Try to avoid stress in the learning situation. Keep the number of incorrect responses down. And always try to correct a child's responses in a way that will introduce the least amount of stress.... Never end the lesson on a sour

note. There will be times when your patience will run short and stress will enter the learning situation. When these situations occur, remember to provide a solution for the child. Show him that he can work his way through the stress situation. This is important ... make sure the child leaves the learning situation with a sense of mastery—not failure and bewilderment."

Now, when I was a child, my experience was the exact opposite: My father or mother would ask a question and then leave my brother and me hanging. If we happened to know the answer we were rewarded by their pleasure. But we felt very stupid and devalued if we did not.

I now realized with shock that I had unconsciously repeated this pattern with my children. I often left them hanging, frustrated, and fearful of their inability to "get it."

Even though I did not mean to repeat this pattern, when it came right down to it, I didn't know any other approach. It was an incredible eye-opener to me that I should actually *give my child the answer!* This is what I learned:

- I should never leave a child hanging.

- Provide a solution before the child becomes stressed.

- Reduce the child's stress by relieving the fear that he will be judged as a failure if he does not know the answer.

- Recognize that learning is not a power-game. It is a process that involves learning how to learn, and feeling grand about it.

My mind was whirling. I knew I was getting closer to a solution for my memorization-challenged children!

Pascal's Experience (10 years old)
Music, Math and Meditation

Here is where my personal experience comes in. I studied and have a degree in music. Because playing an instrument should be as natural as breathing, it is said that musicians must start when they are very young, at a time when the tracks are still being laid in their minds. The earlier the better.

I did not however learn my main instrument when I was a young child. I had a bit of piano and I sang all day long, but I wasn't allowed to have lessons on the instrument of my choice. I began to study seriously at the age of 17, but was nonetheless able to achieve excellence over the next five years. I did this by using techniques from yoga and meditation, both of which I had begun in my teens. I found that when my mind was calm and my energies "in flow" I could engrave musical learning processes onto my deeper mind substance, making progress in leaps and bounds. To use the analogy of the record player, my needle was stable and my mind was smooth. There were no scratches and no static. I could do what is generally considered impossible: learn an instrument as an adult.

Having thus seen for myself that it was possible to lay new tracks as an adult, I wondered if I could modify these methods and make them accessible to my school-age children. Perhaps they, too, could rewrite their math-grooves and achieve excellence.

My second son, Pascal, was in the third grade and at the lower end of his class in math. He was demoralized and angry at himself for not having paid better attention in the first and second grades. He *really* did not like the fact that he wasn't good at math. It made him feel stupid in the eyes of his classmates.

Now, I had sat together with Pascal a couple times and done a modified version of the white light meditation in which the room and the body are filled with light. In the light, we imagined feelings of peace and harmony. (We did not do this as a religious exercise, though it can be done as a kind of prayer—see my book "The Lord's Prayer through the 7 Chakras.")

Because Pascal seemed to feel at ease with such visualization, I thought I could use it as part of our math meditation. One day, when my other three children were out of the house with their father, Pascal and I spent two full hours experimenting. *Math by Grace* was born!

The results were amazing! Immediately after the session and for weeks and months to come, the same answers that had previously eluded him now appeared effortlessly, lightning-fast. In class, he was now second only in math to a highly gifted boy. As a side effect, his handwriting and spelling improved as well.

Pascal asked me to do MBG with him several times in the weeks that followed—once for higher multiplication tables, once for the lower tables, once for division, once to learn division with remainders, and once to learn to add long numbers together. MBG worked. The tracks he laid went straight from question to answer without distraction, befuddlement, or fear of failure.

I was thrilled at the results, both as a mother and as the inventor of *Math by Grace*. However, it wasn't clear to me whether MBG would produce the same results with other children, so I kept my enthusiasm to myself.

Kathryn's Experience (8 years old)

Math and Relaxation

Three years later, my daughter (and youngest child) was in the second grade and showing signs of following in the steps of her older brothers. This was especially disappointing as she'd been enthusiastic about doing addition and subtraction when she was three and four years old. I have to add that my brother is a math teacher and my father was an engineer. I had hoped that at least one of my children might inherit a little of their talent. In any case, although she was only eight years old at the time, I decided that MBG was worth a try.

Now, Kathryn was a cheerful, upbeat child, in love with animals and always on the go. I never doubted her intelligence, though she did not often stand still long enough to demonstrate it. She did not take school very seriously and she often neglected to remember her homework. Years later, when she was at the top of her class and the joy of her teachers she would tell me that she'd assumed in the second grade that she must not be very smart and that she wouldn't have much of a future because she wasn't doing as well as others in her class, particularly in math. She attributes her success to *Math by Grace.*

Because Kathryn was young and I had not done much visualization with her, I decided to base her MBG session on simple relaxation and visualization. I asked her to lie on her back and breathe deeply, to feel the earth rising up beneath her, and then to imagine she was gently floating on a white cloud in the sky. I asked her to envision the whole room as a shiny white cloud.

But—how did I get my wild little girl to lie still?

It helped that Pascal told her MBG worked. He promised her that she would be good at math afterwards. With that incentive, she decided to *bear with Mom* and do what was asked of her—and with *only two sessions, she ascended to the top of her class.*

As mentioned before, Kathryn was a child who appeared to have ADHD and who had not done well in the first or second grade. But when we did *Math by Grace* in the second semester of second grade *she learned how to learn* without static or interference. Once her mind had that experience—once she claimed this learning process as her own—she could apply it to many fields. She improved in all her subjects, began to learn a musical instrument and excelled at that, too.

Kathryn became expert in laying tracks straight from the question to its answer. Today, no matter what she has to learn "by heart" she can do it with far less effort than other children in her class—or so she tells me, always a bit astonished by the fact.

Getting "into flow" with Math

How wonderful, when asked a question, to have the answer appear instantly and effortlessly in one's mind. When learning an instrument, a musician also wants to have no static or interference. We want to see the notes on the page and instantly grasp their musical meaning. We want the fingers and body to instantaneously translate what has been understood into sound. This is called "being one with one's instrument."

There is an emotional reward in it, too. When a musician is one with her instrument and can experience playing with a sense of effortlessness, she plays without fear of making mistakes. In that state, she is filled with joy.

In sport, the same pure concentration has been called "being in flow." Pure, sustained concentration provides a sense of effortlessness, of being one with the sport activity. Sports-persons, after winning a tournament such as downhill skiing, frequently say "It *all just worked*," and that they "*were filled with joy.*"

My children discovered this same joy when we did *Math by Grace*. I treasure the memory of the day Pascal came home radiant from school, saying, "I'm so happy."

"Why?" I asked.

"Because I understand the new stuff in math!"

Martin's Experience (11 years old)
Children with Learning Problems

My son Martin had significantly delayed speech development. With speech therapy, he was able to catch up pretty well in his use of language, but problems understanding and retaining complex information remained. For instance, he could read fluently but then not remember what he had read. The experts that diagnosed him said that he could go to a standard school and that he was capable of learning all the material, but, they said, because he needed additional one-on-one help, a special education class was preferable.

Due to his speech delay, Martin had two years of Kindergarten. His Special Ed class expanded the first grade level into two years as well. This put him three grades lower in school than his age group and that made him feel ashamed.

I had hoped that the Special Ed class would be a good solution for Martin, but one day in July, during the summer vacation that followed second grade, I was shocked to discover that he could not multiply. He understood the principle but could not even recall his "2s" reliably! When it came to the "3s" and beyond he was lost.

I knew he had learned the multiplication tables in class the previous year in school—I had helped him with his homework. So why would 3 x 4 now cause him to start guessing? I was extremely upset with his teacher and with the school system that had allowed this to happen. He *had* the ability to learn this material. *What had gone wrong?*

One day in early October, a few weeks after school had begun again, I sat down with Martin while he did his math homework. To my surprise, he was comfortable in multiplication and knew many solutions "by heart." I sighed with relief and my heart did a little dance of joy. His teacher had finally given him the extra help that he needs! Overwhelmed with gratitude, I immediately phoned to thank her. But before I could say anything, she thanked me! She said, "You really worked hard with Martin on his multiplication tables over the summer. The difference is extraordinary."

"But, I didn't work with him."

"That's strange. Martin says that you worked with him."

"I don't think so."

I went to Martin, quite bewildered, and asked if I had worked with him on math during the summer.

"Yes, one time," he said.

I remembered—I had done *Math by Grace* with him. We had only worked through a few problems because he has a limited attention span. I had forgotten all about it. Now, back in school, he had taught himself the rest—no wonder his teacher thought I had worked with him a lot. Normally, it requires many hours of work to see that kind of improvement!

That is when it hit me—one session of *Math by Grace* with my child who has significant learning problems was enough to move him into a new mode of learning. I had not taught him the answers, but I had *showed him how to lay the tracks*. His subconscious mind had taken the cue and gone with it from there.

I was thrilled about this method that had helped Martin achieve so much, and with so little effort! I thought—quick, write it down! Other parents should know about this!

I sat on my computer for three long days until the first draft of this book was done! I now knew: Each of my three concentration-challenged children had seen significant and unexpected benefits with *Math by Grace*. It was worth telling others about.

Part Two

Preparation for a Math by Grace Session

An Overview

There are three steps involved in a *Math by Grace* session.

- Both the child and the guide **relax** using a combination of relaxation techniques, deep breathing, and guided visualization.

- The guide calmly speaks the math problem and the solution *on the child's exhalation*, and the child innerly **records** the information.

- The guide and child interact in a non-stressful manner in coordination with breathing patterns to **repeat what has been recorded**.

Here, in Part One, I talk about guided visualization and relaxation. Recording and repetition are discussed in Part Three.

Create a Relaxed Space

Choose a place for the session where your child feels relaxed and secure. Good options might be the parent's bed, a favorite sofa, and a blanket spread on the floor of a safe-feeling room. The child's bed is probably not a good idea, especially not for the first try. This is where she is used to entertaining her own thoughts and feelings. It may be hard for her to detach from that. The area in front of an entertainment center such as television or computer is unsuitable for the same reason.

You should feel comfortable. The room does not have to be impeccably tidy but it will not help if, in the middle of the exercise, you are overcome by the feeling that you really should vacuum the floor, dust that table or change the bedding. Use your own sense of comfort, order, and cleanliness as a guide.

To signal that this space is now being used for something special it may be helpful to close the curtains, light a candle, or put a blanket over the TV.

These signals may be equally important for you and your child. Children register changes in our mind-set and attitude and go into the new *inner space* that you provide. Any change in your environment that helps *you* become more centered and calm is what you will be looking for.

Shut Out the World

You will enter a heightened state of awareness during the session. Especially if you already meditate, do yoga or other relaxation exercise, you will find that the deep, calm, regular breathing will quickly help you become more centered, sensitized and focused.

Let your environment support you when you begin to feel and think in a more subtle manner. Make sure no visitors are expected, and that friends who feel free to drop by know they should stay away. Put a "Please Do Not Disturb" sign on your front door. Turn off the phone, computer and fax.

This is an hour devoted to only one thing—re-imprinting the tracks of math in your child's mind.

Invite Your Child

Depending on your child's personality, you can surprise him with the MBG session or prepare him by telling him a day or two in advance that you are going to do something with him that will be new. Tell him for instance that *Math by Grace* will be easy but will take a bit of time, and that the only thing he has to do is to listen just like to a story.

When the time arrives, invite him to lie down on the bed, sofa or floor while you turn down the lights and close the curtains. It need not be dark, but there should be no glares or beams of light to distract. Sit close by, preferably on the same level: if he is on the floor, you are on the floor, if he is on the bed, you are on the bed, if he is on the sofa, you are on the sofa or on a chair nearby.

Relaxation, Visualization, Meditation

Relaxation, visualization and meditation are similar but not the same. Be clear about your strengths in all three areas and design a form of MBG that is right for you and your child.

The age of your child will have an influence on the relaxation exercises and visualization you develop, as will his or her ability to lay still for a longer or shorter time. It is not possible to generalize which approach works for any age-group, however, because every child is unique. Consider this: The exercises you decide upon should help your child relax. They will bring his mind into another state where he is more receptive.

I found that a quick relaxation exercise mixed with simplified visualization worked well for my eight year old daughter. For my older children, a more thorough visualization helped the child go deeper.

Remember—this book is written for parents who have already worked to achieve more calm and focus in their lives with relaxation techniques, yoga, meditation, or other similar paths. When you develop a MBG session for your child, you will be referencing your own experience and taking the age, personality and concentration issues of your child into consideration.

If you do not have this kind of background, look for someone who does to be your child's guide. For instance, check out hypnotherapists, holistic practitioners, yoga or Qigong teachers in your area, and inquire into their background with guided visualization and their interest in helping children. Hopefully you will find someone qualified who will want to explore the techniques described in this book with your child.

If you are your child's guide, become familiar with the basic techniques of MBG. Practice deep relaxation of your body, practice visualization of light along with the release of tension, and become accustomed to the practice of deep, regular breathing. I will discuss these elements in the following pages. Make time every day for these practices, for instance, before going to sleep or upon waking in the morning. Do this for a few weeks before beginning MBG with your child.

Visualization of Light

The visualization of light can be the basis of relaxation, prayer, visualization, and meditation. Mystics from both the east and the west explain that so-called "white light" is always with us, even if we are not aware of it. Some call it the light of our own higher consciousness, and some call it the light of God's love. Some say that these are different expressions for the same thing.

Those who have near death experiences report that they see themselves surrounded in white or golden light. They see beloved persons inside the light. The light is dazzling, liberating, and it conveys a great sense of being loved.

Whether this final vision is a trick of the brain or a spiritual truth is not relevant to the *Math by Grace* method. One thing is clear: Our brains associate white light with liberation and joy. White light wipes the slates of the body-mind clean, freeing us emotionally. It makes us open to record new grooves and helps us lay new tracks.

I personally did not talk to my children about a religious or mystical background to the white light exercise. I felt that it would only excite, confuse or frighten them. MBG should not be scary, exciting or mystifying. It is not about mysticism, religion or occultism—it is about a calming practice of the mind and heart that facilitates learning.

Introduction to the White Light Visualization

This is the basic visualization that I learned from my first meditation teacher, Joseph Koperski, in the early 1970s. A modified form of this meditation has served me well through many decades of life as I describe in my book, "The Lord's Prayer through the 7 Chakras."

You may want to purchase the MBG audiobook on which I recite the visualizations and MBG procedures. You might also record these texts yourself by reading them into your computer or other recording device for your own practice before working with your child. The recording is not meant to replace your speaking the exercises directly to your child, however, for this reason: the guide has to match her speaking to the child's breathing. The guide also should be aware of how the child is feeling, and must possibly say something calming and affirming at any given moment to relax the child.

Below, I describe the basic White Light Visualization. Later in this chapter, I describe child-appropriate modifications.

Basic White Light Visualization

o   Sit crossed-legged on the floor or chair. If you cannot sit cross-legged easily, sit on a chair with legs uncrossed, feet flat on the floor. Place your hands on your thighs, palms up.

o   Breathe deeply and slowly three times.

o   Shake your hands gently to release any tension and place them on your thighs again.

o   Ask that your mind and heart be open to the vision of the White Light. You can ask now that "Healing White Light," or

"Light of Protection," or "Light of Love and Peace" come to you and enter the room where you are sitting.

o Envision the Light entering your room, rising up from the floor to the ceiling and filling the room. It is flowing in a circular motion. It leaves no space unfilled. It lights beneath the furniture, the tables and beds, behind all the furniture and curtains, even in the drawers and closets. The White Light fills the room and penetrates the walls, doors, and windows, filling the corners and pressing up to the ceiling. It is a light of protection and it brings us: Peace, Love, Harmony, Balance, Self-control, and Understanding.

o Breathe deeply and feel the energetic change in the room and around your body. Envision now the light circling one inch around your body, from your feet to your head. Envision the light circling five inches around your body. Now envision the light circling ten inches around your body.

o Feel the closeness of the light, with its peace and love, and feel the release of negative emotions and physical tensions. If you would like, shake your hands gently to release any tension or congested energy. Imagine that this energy turns into dust.

o Ask that the light enter your body through the top of your head. Envision the light circling down through your body until you reach your feet. As you return, pause at the hips. Now gently bring the light back up circling through the trunk of the body, through the neck, and into the head and forehead. Feel again the qualities of Peace, Love, Harmony, Balance, Self-Control, and Understanding. It is here, in this light-filled, clear space behind the forehead, that you can now begin the *Math by Grace* session.

○ When you and your child have completed your MBG session, feel the light again in the forehead, and then circle down again through the body, all way into your feet. Stay there for a few moments. Flex the muscles of your body. Feel the earth beneath you—feel your weight solidly on the place where you sit or lie. It is very important that you complete the session by bringing the energies solidly back into the body in this way.

As Joe Koperski taught the meditation, the light was channeled into the physical body and circled through the chakras. If you have experience in energy work, you may wish to experiment with Joe's basic process. However, teaching or discussing spiritual or energetic experience is beyond the scope of this book, which will only focus on the question: how is the basic white light exercise useful in helping one's child become receptive to laying new tracks for math?

With my own children, I saw that imagining white light at the beginning of the session worked. The image of light is pretty. My children liked it and responded to it, saying that the light made them feel good. Most importantly, the white light visualization tends to clean one's energetic slate from negative emotion—and to relieve children of anxiety. It tends to open the psyche to positive experiences—just what we are looking for here.

If the white light exercise is new to you, try it when you are alone at a quiet time during the day or at night before going to sleep. It is best for an adult to practice this exercise while sitting upright; otherwise, you may dose off.

Whether the light you see is white, off-white, slightly yellow, green, lavender or silver does not matter. Even if you see nothing at all, it is fine. Some people sense the light rather than see it. Find out what works for you.

When you do the white light meditation exercise, try to consciously imagine and feel the qualities of Peace, Love, Harmony, Balance, Self-Control, and increased Human Understanding. This will lift your energy state.

You may also want to check out my book "The Lords Prayer through the Seven Chakras" which explores the White Light Meditation in more detail.

Let's Share....

I am going to share with you how I personally experience the different steps that Joe Koperski developed for this meditation.

Perhaps my experiences will help you evaluate your own responses.

1) Joe would tell us to inhale and exhale slowly three times. I always find that this conscious act of breathing moves me into increased receptivity and a quieter state of mind. It's amazing how quickly it can happen. The breath contains energy, so-called prana. When we breathe consciously, we take more of this energy into ourselves, and when we consciously *intend* to move into a more meditative state, the prana prepares and balances our energy bodies for meditation.

2) Joe would say to imagine light entering the room, rising from the floor to the ceiling. I like this image—it prompts my mind to sense the place in which I sit as a three-dimensional space, and this seems to have a sensitizing effect on the nerves of my body and an opening effect on my mind. Imagining light filling the room is accompanied by a sense of relief and renewal, as if I'm suddenly able to let go of worries and emotional burdens. Sometimes though I become aware of dark emotions and burdens that are deep in my body or that have settled into the physical environment (room, building). The light shows it to me. I no longer suppress it, and I trust that, during meditation, these darker states will lighten up and resolve as much as is possible at this time.

Through these initial steps of breathing and visualization, one's mind enters a heightened state of receptivity. Initially, it may be necessary for an adult to repeat this exercise many times over a span of several days in order to feel a reaction to the light. Adults are not as sensitive as children—our minds may need much practice to grasp the light-experience. After a while, it should begin to register as a real, inner experience. Even if it does not, however, trust the image for *Math by Grace*, as children have an easier time 'getting' the light.

3) Joe would say that when the light has filled the room, it now surrounds the body. It helps to imagine the light especially bright a few inches around us. This image conveys a strong sense of protection. It also moves the mind to sense the three-dimensionality of the body, and to help us get in touch with our physical being. Very often, we perceive our body as if looking in a mirror—we only really *feel* the front of our body. We have no sense for where our backside is—unless something hurts. When the perception of three-dimensionality is trained, the mind becomes overall more alive and subtle in its perception.

When you call on the light—for it is a kind of invocation—you might make it personal. Name the light something that makes sense to you. For instance, ask for the White Light of Healing, or the White Light of Protection, the White Light of Higher Self, or for God's Sacred White Light. Experiment with different names and see if the quality you feel with each is slightly different.

4) Joe would have us imagine light concentrated above the head and then entering the body through the top of the head in a circular motion. It travels down to the feet and then returns back to the head. The exact path it follows is: down through the head, filling out the back of the head as well, down through the neck and into the shoulders, relaxing the muscles there, down into the arms, past the elbows and into the hands and fingertips, wait a moment, feel it tingling there, and then return back to the shoulders. Now the light travels down through the trunk of the body, circling the

spine, nourishing the organs, and into the hips. It travels down through the legs, into the feet and toes, and out through the feet. Then it returns into the feet, and travels back up through the legs and body into the head, where it stays as you sense the light all throughout your body.

I always feel that as the light goes through my body, I can sense where the flow of the light is blocked, or where it encounters tension or suppressed feelings. I dwell in those areas until I feel that something has released and cleared up. At times, my neck will involuntarily move in one direction or the other, as if adjusting itself. My spine may stretch, lift and straighten of its own accord.

I feel then as though I am younger. My nerves are both activated and relaxed. Joe often said that we are charging our cells—and that's just what it feels like. This heightened energy is the basis of the receptive, calm state of mind that makes *Math by Grace* possible.

The White Light Exercise and your Child

You can use the full white light visualization or a modified form with your child, as described in the next section. What you choose will depend on your own meditative preferences and on your child's age and ability to do more complex visualization.

If you decide to do the full exercise with your child, you can practice it with him before bedtime in a matter of minutes— children visualize much faster and more easily than adults. If your child is not ready for this exercise, try a modified version as described in the next two sections.

Modified White Light Exercise I—Floating on a Cloud

The guide and child imagine that white light is entering the room, filling out all the spaces, even under the bed, behind the desk, in the closet. This visualization may require only a minute—excellent for children with a short attention span.

Now ask your child to imagine that she is floating on a cloud of light. Even faster is to simply imagine with your child that the room is filled with a white shiny cloud, and that you are both floating on it.

Now ask your child to breathe deeply three times, and to keep with the image of floating on a cloud. Remember to close your eyes and breathe in and out deeply and slowly three times with your child before starting.

Modified White Light Exercise 2—Floating on a River

In this exercise, the white light is imagined filling the room, and then the child is told that she is floating on a gentle river of light. The water is flowing all around her, from her head to her feet. With the Light, she feels Peace, Love, and Harmony....

In each of these exercises, the child comes to sense her body and mind as being open and free-floating. Once this is achieved, the white light, (cloud or river), is not mentioned again—unless the child is showing signs of tension. Then the image can be brought back to her mind, and she can again be floating on a river or cloud.

Physical Relaxation –

Feeling the Earth beneath Her

It may be helpful to begin your MBG session with a short relaxation exercise. If your child is hyperactive or emotionally stressed, you may want to regularly practice a deep relaxation technique with him before he sleeps. Then you can do an abbreviated form of this exercise before beginning the MBG session.

Autogenic Training

Autogenic Training was developed by the German psychiatrist Johannes Schulz in the early 20th century as an attempt to translate the meditative experience of yoga into a method that the western mind could more easily work with. It was used both to reduce stress and as a form of self-hypnosis: while deeply relaxed, people would give themselves suggestions such as "I will stop smoking" or "I will lose weight."

In a sense, *Math by Grace* is also a form of self-hypnosis[1]. The child is not actually hypnotized by the parent, but both are in a state of mind that is similar to hypnosis—open, formable, and with access to the subconscious mind.

Autogenic Training is done laying on a hard surface such as a blanket spread on the floor. The person concentrates on one part of her body at a time, innerly repeating the suggestion: my (body

---

[1] Some might argue that a child should not experience anything close to hypnosis, as it robs him of his own will power. However, this doesn't happen with *Math by Grace*. The child himself is always present; he is always participating, and is applying his will to math.

part) is getting heavier…, heavier…, heavier. After all parts of the body feel heavier, the person goes through each part of the body again, saying: my (body part) is getting warmer…, warmer…, warmer.

The muscles relax with the suggestion of "heavier" and the blood vessels dilate and allow more blood circulation with the suggestion of "warmer," leading to still deeper relaxation.

The parts of the body are usually mentioned in the following order: Right arm, right leg, left leg, left arm, head, neck, torso, hips.

Suggestion: learning a relaxation technique is easier under the guidance of an experienced teacher. Attending a class can give you a more thorough understanding of the method. DVDs and online courses are also available.

Eutony

Eutony was developed by Gerda Alexander, a German-Danish teacher, in the early 20th century. Eutony is becoming increasingly popular. It requires more time than Autogenic Training to do properly, and must be learned under the guidance of a specially trained guide—a eutonist. With Eutony, we again feel our way into each part of the body, but instead of receiving a suggestion, such as that we are heavier, or warmer, we concentrate instead on the actual physical sensation of the body lying on the floor.

"Feel where the skin of your right arm touches the floor. Feel your way through your skin down into the floor."

By concentrating on taking contact with the floor, we *re-school both the nerves in the body and our attitude toward the physical world.* Usually, we are in a defensive mode of self-protection that extends into our nerves and muscles which are therefore tight and constricted. Unconsciously, we avoid contact with our physical environment. Eutony teaches awareness of the feel of the body in fluid connection with its environment. When we become aware of the flow of energy between ourselves and what we touch, this unconscious defensive mode is re-programmed. Instead of pulling away from contact with the world, the body opens up to it. The physical sign of this opening is that we are suddenly aware of the body's natural weight and that muscles lengthen and relax— because we are no longer pulling away from the world.

Eutony must be learned from a teacher. Gentle stretching and realigning exercises require a therapist's hands to execute. Although I could not use Eutony directly with my children, as I am not a eutonist, some of its components were useful. I would tell my child, "Feel where your body is lying on the floor. Start at your head, and slowly move down to your feet." This helped him to quickly relax.

One of the loveliest experiences in a Eutony session occurs when the body has taken complete contact with the floor and the individual feels their natural weight for the first time. The guide then says, "Feel how the earth rises up beneath you to carry you."

This image also can be used with children. "You are heavy, heavy, heavy. The earth carries your body. Feel how it rises up beneath you and carries your body." This image and the effect it triggers are very reassuring.

A Note about Breathing

In each of these exercises, your child can become aware of her breath. Encourage her to notice when her breathing becomes deeper and slower. If she lays her hands on her abdomen, just below her navel, she can feel her stomach rising up and down as her breath enters and leaves her body.

In Phase Three she will coordinate keeping her breathing steady while she speaks the math answers. Her breathing should remain steady and slow, even when she knows the answer and would like to say it in a hurry.

By having to give the answer slowly she keeps her mind 'smooth' and open, so that the math can become more deeply and smoothly engraved. Later, she will be able to give lightening-fast answers.

From Page 51:

During exhalation, our mental state naturally becomes more relaxed and receptive. During inhalation, we typically become tense and ready for action. Speak the problems only while your child exhales. This helps counteract any tension that your child may feel with learning and memorizing math.

Part Three

The 1, 2, 3's of Math by Grace

You, the parent or guide, will now develop a unique approach to MBG that is tailored to you and your child. Your approach will be based on your background in relaxation, energy work, meditation, etc, and on your child's age, maturity, attention span and other factors such as ADHD or autism. There are no hard and set rules; many variations are possible.

You will want to consider:

- Whether to work with a full or with a modified White Light Visualization; which deep relaxation exercise is best for your child, and whether exercises from your unique background can be incorporated to help you and your child relax and enter another state of mind.

- The amount of time spent in entirety on the session. I have done as long as two hours at one time, but a 20-30 minute session may be all that is tolerated and all that is necessary. Some children may do fine with even shorter sessions.

- The amount of time you spend with each of the three phases. Generally, the older or more mature the child, the longer the attention span and the more time you can spend with each phase. Younger children may need very little time to relax (as much as they can relax) and to initiate the White Light Visualization. Older children may need longer to get into it. You will probably find that your child can concentrate for a somewhat longer time while doing MBG due to the relaxation exercises and visualization, but you'll want to plan realistically so as not make your child feel uncomfortable.

The Three Phases of Math By Grace

1) RELAX

- Sit and lie on the same level.
- Position the child's hands upon his lower abdomen. Talk about deep slow breathing.
- Breathe in and out three times together.
- Lead your child through relaxation and visualization.

Position: You sit, while your child lies down on his back preferably on the same level with you: bed/bed; floor/floor; sofa/chair. When lying, your child places his hands on his lower abdomen, just beneath the navel, to better feel his inhalation and exhalation. Ask your child to breathe in and out deeply three times together with you. After that, remind your child occasionally that his breath should be slow and easy. Remember, children naturally breathe more quickly than adults, as their lungs are smaller.

If you are going to do a special relaxation exercise, integrate it into MBG now.

Lead your child through one of the White Light Visualization exercises. You will hopefully both feel content, happily apart from the world. Of course, if your child tends to be hyperactive, she may still exhibit some restlessness, but she is doubtless doing her best to participate and her mind is becoming more receptive for MBG.

2) RE-IMPRINT

- Explain to your child that you will speak a math problem, along with its solution, while your child is exhaling. Ask your child to listen, and to then imagine writing the problem along with the solution. She might want to imagine writing on a chalkboard, and that the back of her forehead is a chalkboard.
- Briefly revisit the White Light image before beginning.
- Coordinate your breathing to match your child as much as possible (a small child will breathe too quickly for this to be strictly doable).
- Speak the problem **with** its solution slowly on one exhalation.
- Give your child time to do her inner work before going on to the next problem.

During the re-imprinting of basic math, *calmly* speak aloud a math **problem and its solution** while keeping an eye on your child's breathing. Speak on your child's exhalation. Your child listens and visualizes the problem and solution in her mind by drawing it on a chalkboard on the inner side of her forehead, writing it with an imaginary pencil in a book that she visualizes, or she may chisel or scratch it into imaginary soft stone or clay.

Consider whether your child would benefit from writing the problem two - three times in her imagination. Give her enough time to do the inner work and then calmly move on to the next problem. Depending on your child's concentration span, it may be possible and desirable to re-imprint inversions as well. For instance, speak: 5 x 6 is 30. Give your child time to write this equation in her mind, and then speak an inversion: 30 divided by 6 is 5. Again, give your child time to write the equation before speaking the second inversion: 30 divided by 5 is 6.

During exhalation, our mental state naturally becomes more relaxed and receptive. During inhalation, we typically become tense and ready for action. Speak the problems only while your child exhales. This helps counteract any tension that your child may feel with learning and memorizing math.

3) REVIEW

- Explain to your child that she will now hear the math problem spoken while she exhales. She should then inhale, with no hurry, and calmly speak the problem with its solution on her next exhalation.
- While the child exhales, the guide speaks the math problem, for instance: 2 x 2.
- The child inhales once, maintaining a relaxed breathing rhythm, and then speaks both the problem and the solution: 2 x 2 is 4.
- Again, the parent inhales in rhythm with the child, and on their next exhalation, the parent speaks, calmly: 2 x 3.
- The child again inhales after hearing the problem spoken, and on her next exhalation speaks both the problem and the solution: 2 x 3 is 6.

Give your child a few moments to relax before beginning. You now speak only the problem, coordinating your speaking as always with your child's exhalation. Your child repeats the problem *with* its solution, without changing her speed of breathing.

You and your child should enjoy speaking calmly while exhaling. Breathing is never hurried. The words are spoken with the same slow pace, even if the child knows the answer and would like to say it faster. There is no rush for the child to give the answer, and no rush for you to pose a new question.

The feeling is one of no pressure whatsoever. Hopefully your child will give the correct answers. If an answer is incorrect, however, or if your child hesitates while looking for the answer, go back to Phase Two and state the question again with the answer. Tell your child to write it again on her inner chalkboard. You might suggest that she write it in a gold color, and that she use an eraser or cloth each time afterwards to clean the slate before writing it again. This kind of fantasy can help bring her deeper into the exercise.

The older or mature child will find it easier to work with his breath. If the younger child does not fully respond to the breathing method, don't force it. Just remember that the calmer you both feel, the better the math will be engraved upon your child's mind. It is this calmness and the total lack of stress that allow the math to become the child's own possession.

Important: If the child does not know the answer, it's okay. The parent should however *immediately* offer the solution, with no criticism attached—and in the same calm manner as before. Repeat again the math problem with its solution, exactly as in Phase Two. Ask the child to innerly repeat the problem and its solution three times, visualizing it on her forehead-chalkboard. There is no hurry.

Now return to Phase Three. Say the problem slowly on your child's exhalation without its solution. This time, your child will provide the correct answer and you can move on. If your child should provide a wrong answer, it may be time to end the MBG session as your child must be tired.

If there are several problems your child hesitates on, create a list or 'repeat pile' to review again after completing the entire third phase.

Slow Repetition Helps the Mind Learn

The slow pace and calm concentration enable the mind to re-imprint math. This same approach, by the way, is used to master a musical instrument: a difficult musical passage that should be played quickly is first practiced at ultra-slow speed many times.

Beginner-musicians often find it difficult to practice in slow motion, but experienced musicians understand that only by practicing slow will they eventually play it fast and flawlessly! Through slow repetition, all urges to rush, and all fears about doing it right or wrong, are overcome. Through slowness, and through cultivating a calm mind, the tracks for playing a passage well are laid straight in the brain. Afterwards, the fingers know what to do automatically and the difficult passage seems to play itself at top-speed. It becomes effortless.

Taking the exercises at a slow pace is key to *Math by Grace*. Watch your child for any change in breathing. Faster or more hectic breathing indicates tension. Help the child relax again, for instance, by giving positive feedback in a calm tone of voice. Then lead the child back to the exercise, without hurry, and without a feeling that she must be good at it.

Even if the child cannot keep to the exercise perfectly, this is the goal to aim for: not right answers, but smooth, calm answers, given without tension.

Flash Cards – So Helpful!

Make a set of flash cards, and go through them until the problems and solutions become familiar to you. (Flash cards have the question on one side, and the answer on the other.) These cards may be helpful when you develop sessions for your child (see pages 56 and 61) as well as when you practice MBG yourself (see next session).

Practice Relaxation and MBG on Yourself

We tend to forget basic math when out of school—a perfect excuse to practice MBG on yourself first, before working with your child. Make flash cards (see above) and review your basic math to ascertain what you still remember and what you have forgotten and need to re-imprint. Prepare either a "repeat-pile" or a write out a list of problems and answers.

Practice one of the relaxation and visualization methods every day. When you go into a deeper and more receptive mind space, guide yourself innerly through a MBG session. Read the problem and its solution. Close your eyes, and, while exhaling, mentally write it onto the chalkboard on the backside of your forehead. Repeat the math problem with its solution three times, all the while keeping your breathing calm and steady. Do inversions, too, if you wish.

You may find MBG more difficult than your child will, for someone else is not guiding you. Being one's own guide makes it harder to relax completely. Still, doing MBG on yourself will give you a sense for how the exercise works with the breathing rhythms and repetitions. And it will help you become more secure in your basic math skills.

Decide on the Scope

How many problems you work through with your child will depend on your child's age, attention span, and other issues. Set your time allowances so that your child does not become tired or stressed. But be prepared: if your child wants to go on for a longer time, be ready to do that as well.

With Pascal, who was nearly ten the first time we tried MBG, I concentrated on the 6s, 7s, 8s and 9s multiplication rows. We went through each row up to 12. Next time, we did the 11s and 12s.

Retrospectively, this was probably too much at one go—but with a family of four young children, it was hard to find a block of time alone at home for MBG. I wanted to take full advantage of those precious two hours!

I thought we had covered the difficult problems and were done, but a week later, Pascal asked me to go through the easy rows with him, the 2s through 5s. He could already do them correctly, but he was not able to do them as lightening-fast as he could now do the harder rows, and he wanted that same good feeling of security at every level of difficulty.

Pascal, I can safely say ten years later, is not naturally gifted for math. He is a dreamy artist. He therefore needed each individual step of basic math gone through with MBG. He then became quite competent and was among the best in math in his class in elementary school. When he was older, he managed to do higher math, but was never really motivated to learn it. However, this could have been influenced by many factors besides his basic math talent—teachers, peer group, and so on.

With my daughter Kathryn, who was eight when we started MBG and who had a very short attention span, I used another method to find our focus. Sitting at the kitchen table, I first went through the multiplication tables with her using a *set of homemade flash cards*. I put aside all those cards that she showed the *slightest* hesitation on. Hesitation means that the track is not straight between the problem and its solution in the brain.

I divided the cards into three shorter MBG sessions. Because she was so young, we could not work on the same time scale as had been possible with Pascal. Her Phase Two time was fairly short, and we reviewed no more than fifteen problems. When we went on to Phase Three, I would again use the cards and note which problems she still hesitated on. Then I went back and repeated Phase Two with her on those problems, using the "repeat pile" of flash cards. Kathryn's skills greatly improved. Within the next two months, she was among the top students in her class—and it was a strong class. She has gone on to study honors math.

Kathryn was lucky. In elementary school and junior high, her school class was dominated by smart, sweet, ambitious girls. The natural competition among them challenged her to do her best. She always got along with her teachers, who respected her natural leadership abilities (what appeared as attention deficit disorder in Kindergarten developed into profound leadership qualities—she became the respected boss of the class, spurring the others on to do their best). I believe that Kathryn's good fortune with her peer group and teachers played a large role in her success. For the best in oneself to develop, both natural ability and a good social environment are necessary.

Martin was nearly eleven when we began MBG. He had significant learning difficulties and was in a Special Ed class. I used flash cards to determine which problems he could do instantly, which problems he hesitated on, and which he did not know at all. I had him draw the problem and solution on the inside of his forehead. Then we moved on to Phase Three. Most of the answers he still did not know, so we went back to Phase Two and I again stated the problem with the solution and had him repeat this with his inner voice three times, drawing it on his inner chalkboard. Using the flash cards with Phase Three, I separated the problems he could now do without hesitation from those he could not, and returned to these, having him repeat them again.

> Never leave a child hanging, searching for an answer. If a child hesitates, immediately provide the answer, and then put the card aside in the 'repetition pile'. The child should at no time feel stressed by actively looking for the answer.

I did not check the results of MBG with Martin. Our work together was so brief that I soon forgot we had done one session during summer vacation. But several weeks later, after school began, I heard from his teacher that my "drilling him over summer vacation" had greatly improved his math skills. She probably thought I had worked with him every day. Apparently, when Martin learned how to memorize math problems and solutions without stress, he was then able to go on and apply the process on his own.

At the time, I knew nothing about autism. I now believe that Martin has a mild form of Asperger syndrome. Read more about how I developed special MBG exercises for him on pages 61-62.

Homework

Math by Grace changed my approach to doing homework with my children. I no longer believed that they should do homework all alone—especially math. I realized that leaving kids alone with math homework would inevitably lead to many moments when the child sits there thinking, "This is hard," or "I want to do something else," or "I didn't understand this completely in school today, and now I feel like a fool."

These inner dialogues become scratches and static so that a child can no longer think clearly or approach a problem with self-confidence. When a parent sits with the child and prevents the static from happening, math again becomes fun. Learning is fun because it jiggles the nerves in the brain, in a similar way that humor does.

Whenever I sensed a hesitation, I would either help the child find a solution or actually provide the solution, in a tone of calm normality. Then I'd ask my child to close her eyes and repeat the problem and solution innerly. Because they had already done MBG with me, they immediately understood what was expected, that the repetition should be done calmly, with clear concentration.

Scrunched Eyebrows

One thing to look for when a child does homework is a scrunched eyebrow. This is a sure sign that a child is working too hard. She is blocking herself with thoughts of: "I have to succeed at this," or, "Gosh this is hard!"

Your child may have other warning signs that you can note. For instance, when her face is tipped to the side and supported by her hand, that might signal: "I am working in a way that is tiring for me."

Mimicking the scrunched eyebrows in a humorous way can help your child become aware of what she is doing. A hand-signal between you and your child can be wiping your own forehead with your fingers. It means: "Wipe away those wrinkles, dear. It's not really so hard—relax, and it will become easier."

One thing I found myself reminding my children is that they should wait for the answer to come to them, and not go looking for it. If the answer does not come quickly, the problem goes to the "repeat pile" for special, MBG attention.

Exercises for my Special Needs Child

I wrote about Martin on pages 27-28 and 57. Martin posed a challenge to the adults, therapists, and teachers who knew him. One-on-one he seemed quite capable, but as soon as several people were present, he appeared unable to connect the dots in whatever was being taught or discussed. His teachers were perplexed. They were not sure to which degree this behavior was laziness. They either underestimated or overestimated him, leaving Martin unsure what was expected of him.

Now, two unfortunate things happened when I was pregnant with Martin. When the pregnancy was three weeks along, my oldest son, Michael, had an accident and went to hospital for two weeks. You can imagine the stress hormones I produced at that time! Then, during the third month of pregnancy, I was ill. I called a doctor to ask if I should bring down the high fever with aspirin or if I should let it stay high to fight the illness. He said he knew of no impact of fever on a baby and that I shouldn't worry about it.

Turns out that he was wrong. High fever in pregnancy is a considerable risk factor for an unborn child's brain development. I also lost a few pounds while ill. Weight loss causes fat-soluble neurotoxins, usually stored in fat cells, to flow out into the blood stream (and also into the baby) when the fat cells "melt."

Martin had a delayed development. Diagnosed at three and a half with the mental development of a nine month old, he was nonetheless smart, funny, sweet, and talented. He could draw beautifully and he was a genius on the drums. But as he grew older and realized that he was disadvantaged, he became sad about himself and sarcastic about others, such as his little sister, Kathryn, who seemed to have it much easier than he did. He felt it was unfair that in spite of trying his hardest, he could not do as well as others.

When he finally was able to do the times tables after our work with MBG, he told me that he wanted to go out of the Special Education class. It just wasn't right for him, he said. Now, along with not having memorized his basic math in the Special Ed class, he had also not learned how to write in cursive longhand. He could write in block letters only. At home, he now began learning how to write in longhand. He practiced every day. We also began learning more about math. I will tell you in a moment how we did that.

Once I saw that Martin was quickly making progress with longhand at home, I contacted a school psychologist. I talked to Martin and said, "If leaving the Special Ed class is what you want, you have to tell her about it in a way that is convincing. Do not expect her to just understand. Explain it."

That day, Martin's eloquence and passion so greatly impressed the school psychologist that she assembled a team to consult about Martin including his speech therapist, his Special Ed teacher, the teacher of the class where he would go if he entered regular school, a school administrator, and me. We decided to aim for Martin's integration into the regular school class. Toward the end of the semester, he would attend regular school for three weeks. If that trial went well, he would enter the regular class the following semester.

It was Martin's job to continue making progress at home so that when he entered his new class he would not be far behind in the basics. We had various booklets that provided exercises for handwriting, and Martin practiced every day, improving quickly. But what about math? What could we do that was tailored to Martin's needs?

I thought it through and came up with an idea—we could work creatively with flash cards in conjunction with MBG, always remembering the calm approach, and the slow rhythm and the breathing.

In the living room at a low coffee table I would lay out one row, say 6s, so that the cards extended in a row, or a tower, away from Martin, with the lowest card nearest him and the highest card farthest away.

What we did was simple but provocative. Rather than leaving the cards in a deck, and randomly calling out one problem after another, we arranged them into a visual structure that would inform the child about the relationship of one problem to the rest of the row.

The cards had either the question or the answer visible, and Martin would read up or down the row, giving always the full response. For instance, if either 42 or 6 x 7 were visible on the card, he would say:

6 x 7 is 42.

And then, the inversions:

42 divided by 7 is 6. 42 divided by 6 is 7.

Sometimes we skipped over cards, reading only every second card, or every third card. This exercise provided a lot of information about the structuring of numbers. I hoped it would reinforce what he had already accomplished through the MBG math visualization, and expand his understanding about math theory through visual information. When he entered regular school, he would be expected to mentally multiply 1s by 10s and soon 10s by 10s, as in 14 x 58. I hoped that this extra work would prepare him, and I believe it did, as he could indeed keep up with math in elementary school. He later had problems with geometry and algebra. He could do the work in class, but a few days later, could hardly recall what he had learned. But at least basic math would stick with him, and *that* is what we need in order to manage our daily lives!

Martin continued to get passing grades. He always encountered the same problem though—teachers who could not quite decide if he was just lazy or if he had a true disability, and who made him feel ashamed. This was very hard on him. He vented his tension with comic imitations of his teachers at the dinner table. We were in stitches!

When he was 17 years old, Martin's last teacher heard him perform one of the complex compositions he had taught himself on piano. Amazed, he organized a presentation to which he invited Martin's classmates and his former teachers. This teacher told me that he just couldn't understand how Martin's creative sides could be so overlooked by his former teachers.

In Europe, there is far less understanding for the range of autism spectrum than here in the US. I never heard the term Aspergers, nor did teachers, therapists, or school psychologists ever mention the possibility of mild autism to me. Martin's teachers did not know how to understand him, and my husband and I were at a loss as well. That said, what Martin accomplished was remarkable. He transferred from a Special Ed class where he clearly was not learning well to a regular school class, first catching up with their level and then holding pace.

Today, Martin is 19 years old. He is attending a Waldorf school that introduces young adults to different job directions while also moving on academically. His grades are good. He goes to school and does his homework with discipline. His creative genius expresses itself on YouTube, in musical compositions.

I hope that this description of the approach I took with Martin's basic math skills will be helpful to parents whose children have similar issues. I was at a loss as to how to help my son achieve what I felt intuitively he could accomplish, and what he needed to accomplish for himself for his self-esteem. I improvised with the tools I had and came up with a method that seemed to work. Maybe this approach will help you and your child as well, or you will improvise and come up with exercises that are better for your child.

Today there is an amazing support system in the US for children with autism, and you may be receiving excellent guidance already. If so, please share this book with your experts. Perhaps they will find MBG useful.

Part Four

Developing Math Abilities with MBG

Improve Your Own Math

If you work with MBG and follow along with your child's homework, the basic math you learned as a child will return to you, probably better than before.

This happened to me. I was unable to do addition into adulthood without counting my way from one number to the next. Why? Because as a child I was not shown how to memorize.

While learning with my children, I was able to re-lay my own math tracks and become a whiz, even with large numbers—and all in my head.

Do Math in Your Head

I did not raise my children in the US. Our family was living abroad in Germany. I would have preferred to home-school my kids, but it is illegal in Germany and in many places in Europe. The good thing though is that I got a firsthand look at what Europeans expect of their kids at school. PISA testing in these countries shows higher math scores than in the US. What do they do differently?

Well, for one thing, they expect children to solve mathematical problems in their heads. My children had both a weekly written and an oral test in math. For the oral test, they were expected to write down the solution to a problem spoken by the teacher—all of the actual figuring was done in their heads.

If kids can do this, it can't be all that hard—right? True! Once the tracks are set, it is easy to do math in one's head at any age—if we practice and stay calm with it.

When my son Pascal was having problems with the addition of tens and hundreds, such as 29 plus 115, I again did MBG with him, this time calmly looking at the positions of numbers—the 1s to the right, the 10s to the left, then the 100s and 1000s.

Thousands. Hundreds. Tens. Ones.

Together, we visualized the addition of large numbers, moving slowly from the 1s to the 10s to the 100s to the 1000s. The problem we had was being able to remember the solution we'd already found once we began to solve the next step. If the solution in the 1s column was a 5, we had to remember that 5, even when we were working on in the 100s or the 1000s.

I recall that while working on this with Pascal, we did not achieve much excellence. Nevertheless, over the following months, Pascal became excellent at adding or subtracting larger figures in his head. *His brain accepted the challenge and worked it out.* And I got better at it as well.

The Mystery of Learning

This experience with Pascal reminds me of what it is like to learn a musical instrument—a mysterious process indeed. One can struggle with a problem—with finger technique, breathing technique, bow technique, musical expression or just getting a beautiful sound—but until a musician has confronted the problem full on, has gone consciously to the very point of the blockade again and again, there will be no breakthrough.

What this looks like is this—a week of playing the same piece over and over, trying to feel your way into the demands of the music, and mostly feeling as though you're getting nowhere. But through the slowness, and by consciously being aware of the problem, the brain recognizes this simple fact: there is a problem to solve. Suddenly, the breakthrough arrives. Progress is made. You do not know exactly what made the difference, but it works. You can now do well what previously seemed impossible.

Again, only by practicing the piece in an extremely concentrated manner (best in slow motion) can the subconscious mind become aware that there is a problem to solve—and through that calm slowness, begin to lay new tracks.

The same thing happened with Pascal: we went into deep relaxation and worked on the addition of large numbers. There was no apparent progress during the time we worked on it. We both felt quite inadequate in fact. But soon afterwards, he became excellent at it.

The same thing happened with my autistic son Martin. While we practiced the 3s with MBG I did not see much improvement. But a few weeks later, he had the 3s down pat. He was then able to apply the same principle on his own and memorize more multiplication problems. His subconscious mind had been confronted with a problem (the necessity to learn math), had been shown a solution (memorization), and had gone ahead and laid down the tracks for it.

Perhaps this is the very secret of the *Math by Grace* approach: it allows a child's subconscious mind to clearly grasp the problem of basic math and the process of memorization.

The Next Steps in the Mastery of Math Basics

So far, I have spoken about learning multiplication and division. The MBG method can also be applied to learning basic addition and subtraction. However, it is important to be sure that your child has actually grasped the principles behind math. For this, putting out numbers of objects such as apples, buttons or nuts on a table in different sized groups for addition, subtraction, multiplication, etc., is necessary. It is senseless to practice MBG if your child has not grasped the principles behind math.

Some children, like Kathryn and Martin, will benefit from only one or two sessions with MBG; their minds 'get' how to memorize, and they go on to work independently. But if your child is like Pascal, you may find yourself implementing MBG for many more steps of basic math.

For instance, Pascal's next challenge was division with remainders. He was strangely confused. If asked: "What is 84 divided by 9?" he would answer that it is 9 remainder 1. He had his wires crossed: instead of counting up from 81 to 84, he would count downwards from the first answer to the next lower tens-number, in this case, from 81 to 80.

Now, as a rational adult, I thought his mistake was so obvious that merely explaining it to him would help him overcome it. But I was wrong. He continued to count downwards instead of upwards, perplexed as to what wasn't right. This was a case where the child had somehow identified himself with the wrong process, or, as Siegfried Engelmann puts it, he had invested some of his self in the wrong approach.

Fortunately, one short MBG session moving through the process of division with remainders solved it. He was now lightening fast in solving simple division with remainders in his head.

Please note: it was necessary to go through the process with him s-l-o-w-l-y while his mind was open and relaxed. This erased his previous program—like reformatting a computer disk—and allowed him to imprint the correct approach with clearly laid tracks in his brain.

Learn More Math in Your Head (Mental Math)

The next important step is the multiplication of 1s and 10s. For instance, 9 x 28. The child first multiplies 9 x 20, which is 180. Then he multiplies 9 x 8, which is 72. He must be able to remember his first answer, 180, and add to it his second answer, 72. My mind now instantly tells me that the answer is 252. I briefly recognize that 8 + 7 is 15, and my brain does the rest, arriving safely from problem to solution.

The next, much more difficult step, is multiplying 10s times 10s. For instance, 47 x 38. Starting with the 1s position of the first number, 7 x 30 is 210, and 7 x 8 is 56. 210 and 56 are 266. (You should reach this answer in your head and write it down or just remember it if you can.) Then, 40 x 30 is 1200, and 40 x 8 is 320, which added together are 1520, which we write down beneath 266, or just remember it. These are added—in the head or on paper, depending on the complexity and length of the problem—and you have the answer, 1786.

Math by Grace in Class?

It is my hope that this book will be read by teachers in primary school, and that it may inspire them to try a new approach in class. I can imagine, for instance, that the teacher has her students lie on mats on the floor while she leads them through a simple relaxation exercise, and then works through one multiplication table in a slow, calm manner, giving both the problem and the solution, and having the children write these on the chalkboard on the inner side of their foreheads. Suggest to the children throughout the exercise that they should breathe deeply and regularly. The children can lie with their hands on their abdomens, so that they feel the gentle rising and falling of their stomach with their inhalation and exhalation.

Another suggestion is that therapists who specialize in deep relaxation visit primary school classes and offer this kind of training.

Where Does This Lead?

A parent may ask herself—will MBG turn my child into a math genius, especially if we begin when she is very young?

Probably not. The true gift for math is rare. But your child will have learned how to learn, and will be able to apply that ability to areas where he or she truly has talents. And by being the best he or she can be at math, the child's self-esteem will be lifted. That, in itself, is a great reward.

A Request

Please place this booklet into the hands of teachers (as well as math teachers of all levels) and therapists.

When more people experiment, and more experiences are available to compare and understand, we can learn better ways to help our children learn.

Resources

When talking with math teachers and math tutors I hear two common complaints: children are not taught the theory behind basic math, and they are not taught how to learn. By the time they are supposed to learn fractions their fundamental understanding for math is overwhelmed and they are blocked from then on.

I have been looking into "The Secrets of Mental Math" by Arthur Benjamin. Reviewers on amazon.com write that this is math as it should have been taught in school. As I read the sections on basic addition, subtraction, multiplication and division, I discovered an exact replica of the way that math is taught to children in Germany: individual mental steps, shortcuts and checks are taught along with easily explained math theory.

I can only recommend buying one of the mental math books for adults. You do not need to learn the fancy stuff, but a review of basic steps will help you help your child get the basics down pat.

Contact Information

I gratefully welcome all feedback, stories, and suggestions. You can reach me at this email address:

feedback@mathbygrace.com

Afterword

After seeing the amazing way that *Math by Grace* helped my concentration-challenged children reach their full basic math potential, (where various drills and games just did not work), the desire grew to publish this book.

I feel confident that the methods described here can help most children—provided the child is willing to open up to his parent or guide and participate.

Nutrition should not be neglected. Food feeds the brain, the nerves, the hormones and the immune system. Refined sugar, additives, and unhealthy fats (found in most packaged foods) and the pesticides found in the fat of animal products (buy animal products organic) do not support a child's optimal development— they undermine it. My daughter Kathryn began to truly excel at school when she stopped eating packaged food, soda and chips at the age of twelve (but she did not stop eating chocolate and that seemed to be okay!). She would like all kids to know about this, as it is obvious to her now what the effect of poor food is on the brain, on mood, and on the ability to maintain stable weight (important especially to a girl) and energy.

Visual media can be detrimental as well. TV, films and computer games keeps the brain working in a certain mode that is not conducive to learning, to memorization or to a more deep understanding of the basic concepts and skills that keep our world functioning. One teacher explained to me that if a child watches television after studying for a test, what he learned will be less accessible to recall. I strongly believe that the use of media should be restricted during the school week—especially in the case of adolescent boys who tend to dive into the world of gaming, and who need to have a social life and a physical life (sports) as well.

If your child has developmental issues, consider looking into the possibility of food and chemical sensitivities. We were able to turn Michael's life around by eliminating certain trigger foods that he tested positive for when he was five years old. A plethora of recipe books show how to cook while avoiding your child's trigger foods. After at least six months of avoidance, the immune system will have had time to recover. Many children and adults overcome their sensitivities and allergies by avoiding their trigger food consequently for a period of time, and then re-introducing the food on a four day rotation diet.

A great resource for information on food and chemical allergies and sensitivities is Dr. Doris Rapp's book, "Is This My Child?" I also recommend Dr. Leo Galland's "Superimmunity for Kids." Galland provides recipes that kids like made from food that they are used to from the standard American diet. I also enjoyed Hilary Jacobson's book "Mother Food" which talks about foods and herbs taken historically to support the mother's and baby's immune systems and to maintain an abundant milk supply.

Math by Grace will soon be available as an audiobook.

About the Author

Dana Williams, a stay-at-home mother of four children, has lived alternately in Europe and the United States. Her hobbies are film, music, yoga and meditation, and horseback riding.

Williams made two remarkable discoveries, both stemming from a form of meditation that she learned from Joe Koperski in Los Angeles in the 1970s. These are published under the titles *"Math by Grace* – Memorization of Basic Math for Concentration-Challenged Children through Relaxation and Meditation Techniques" and "The Lord's Prayer, the Seven Chakras, the Twelve Life Paths – the prayer of Christ consciousness as a light for the auric centers and map through the paths of astrology."

9 780979 599552